20TH CENTURY MEDIA

1920s & 30s
ENTERTAINMENT FOR THE PEOPLE

20TH CENTURY MEDIA – 1920s & '30s
was produced by

David West 👫 **Children's Books**
7 Princeton Court
55 Felsham Road
London SW15 1AZ

Picture Research: Carrie Haines
Designer: Rob Shone
Editor: James Pickering

First published in Great Britain in 2002 by
Heinemann Library, Halley Court, Jordan Hill,
Oxford OX2 8EJ, a division of Reed Educational and
Professional Publishing Limited.

OXFORD MELBOURNE AUCKLAND
JOHANNESBURG BLANTYRE GABORONE
IBADAN PORTSMOUTH (NH) USA CHICAGO

06 05 04 03 02
10 9 8 7 6 5 4 3 2 1

ISBN 0 431 15252 7 (HB)
ISBN 0 431 15266 7 (PB)

British Library Cataloguing in Publication Data

Parker, Steve, 1952-
20th century media 1920s & 30s: entertainment for
the people
1. Amusements - History - Juvenile literature
I. Title II. Twentieth-century media 1920s & 30s
790'.09042

Printed and bound in Italy

PHOTO CREDITS :
Abbreviations: t-top, m-middle, b-bottom, r-right,
l-left.

Cover - all - Corbis Stock Market. 3, 5br, 6tr, 7tr, 10tr,
16br, 21bl, 22tr, 24tr, 24-25, 25tr, 26bl & m, 27l -
Mary Evans Picture Library. 4mr, 11tr, 29br - The Art
Archive. 4br, 18 both, 19br, 20 both - The Kobal
Collection. 4b, 23ml - The Culture Archive. 5t, 6bl, 6-
7m, 7br, 8 both, 9ml, 10bl & br, 11l & br, 12-13t,
13tr, 17ml & mr, 18-19, 19tr, 21br, 22m, 24b, 26ml,
28t, 29tr - Popperfoto. 5bl - The Art Archive/Eileen
Tweedy. 9tr & br, 12tr, 12-13b, 14 all, 15tl & tr, 16l,
17t, 22bl, 25m, 26tr & 28b - Hulton Archive. 13br -
The Advertising Archive Ltd. 20-21 - AKG. 23r - Bell
Laboratories. 27br (t) - Fabian Bachrach/Reader's
Digest. 27br (b) - Bradford Bachrach/Reader's Digest.
27br - Reader's Digest. 29bl - The Art Archive/British
Library.

*The dates in brackets after a person's name
give the years that he or she lived.*

*An explanation of difficult words can be
found in the glossary on page 30.*

20TH CENTURY MEDIA

1920s & 30s

ENTERTAINMENT FOR THE PEOPLE

Steve Parker

Heinemann
LIBRARY

CONTENTS

BOOKS FOR ALL

In 1936 Penguin Books started a new trend in publishing – paperbacks. They were inexpensive enough for ordinary people to buy, unlike hardbacks.

'WIRELESS'

Radio brought a whole new world of listening pleasure, from news and sports to opera and theatre, right into people's homes. This advertisement for the latest radio set dates from 1928.

NO LONGER SILENT

Movies were 'silent', with only musical accompaniment, until 1927. Then singer Al Jolson amazed the world by speaking directly from the screen. 'Talkies' had arrived.

INSTANT MEDIA

We find out what happens in the world, through the media. They provide news, knowledge and entertainment. We have many forms of media today, the newest being the Internet. In 1920, as people recovered from World War One, there were fewer forms. Newspapers were the main medium for spreading news.

WORLD AT WAR – AGAIN
World War Two broke out in 1939. The media played a greater part than ever before, in spreading news and shaping opinion.

Radio was just beginning. There was no television. Cinema was established but movies were 'silent', with no sounds directly from the screen. The next 20 years saw huge changes. By 1940, radio was a dominant force, with instant news. Movies had sound. Television sets were creeping into homes. Technology was racing ahead and media businesses boomed. Sadly, some things did not change, and the world was again plunged into war.

'COUCH POTATOES' OF 1935
Even in the early days of radio and television, fears arose that these media might become too powerful. Would people laze about, listen and watch, and be told what to think, with no views of their own?

MORE MAGAZINES
Magazines began to expand from about 1920, carrying a mix of news reports, in-depth analysis of events, features and fiction. Fortune was founded in 1930.

GREATEST SHOW ON EARTH

Every four years sees the greatest sports event in the world – the Olympic Games. The Games bring together athletes of all nations in peace and harmony. At least, they should. But several times, media coverage of the Games has been used for less peaceful purposes.

HIJACKED

World events like the Olympics create massive public interest and media coverage. On occasion this has been 'hijacked' by a cause which is not closely connected with the Games, or even sport. In 1936 the Olympic venue was Berlin, Germany. The German nation was under control of the Nazi movement, led by Adolf Hitler.

ON YOUR MARKS …
Jesse Owens and his rivals start the 100-metre sprint final.

SUPREME DREAM
Strength, physical prowess and discipline were glorified by the Nazis.

ON VIEW TO THE WORLD

Millions of people were reading about the Games in newspapers and magazines, listening on radio, and watching on newsreel film. Hitler saw an ideal opportunity to tell the world about Nazi supremacy. Germany had used every means possible to build its athletics team, with the latest scientific advances and training methods. The aim was to dominate the Games and thereby show how powerful and successful the Nazi movement had become.

6

SALUTE THE GAMES

At the Olympic opening ceremony in Berlin, Adolf Hitler (fifth from left) and his senior officials gave the raised-arm Nazi salute. This had nothing to do with the Games. But it appeared in newsreel films and photographs all over the world.

ARYANS IN THE MEDIA

Nazis believed in the destiny of the Aryan race. These were German people who were strong, fit and intelligent, who followed their leader without question and would die for him, who were destined to rule others, and who were white. German newspapers, films, books, works of art and other media were used to spread the idea of Aryan greatness.

'Perfect' Aryans in Family, painted by Wolf Willrich.

GOLDEN IMAGE

As Owens received his gold medal, Hitler left in anger – not at all the spirit of the Olympic Games.

7

ANGRY EXIT

Germany did indeed win more medals than any other nation. But Hitler's racist dreams of supremacy backfired. As the world watched through the media, US athlete Jesse Owens became the undisputed star of the Games. He won four gold medals, for the 100- and 200-metre sprints, long (broad) jump, and as a member of the 400-metres relay team. Hitler was furious that a black athlete should beat the cream of his white-only Aryan team, and he stormed out of the stadium.

RADIO'S GOLDEN AGE

During World War One (1914–18), radio broadcasting by the public was banned in many countries, so it did not interfere with radio's secret use by the military. At the same time, as often happens in war, the technology of radio leaped ahead.

READY TO GROW

By 1920, wartime bans were being lifted and radio was set to spread like wildfire. Many small stations sprang up, especially in the USA and Britain, followed by the rest of Europe. One of the first station licences was granted to Westinghouse's Frank Conrad, for Radio KDKA in Pittsburgh, USA. This brought news of America's 1920 presidential election, updated faster than any newspaper could manage.

HOME OF THE 'BEEB'
Broadcasting House became the home of BBC Radio in 1932. This prestigious office building in Central London was a symbol of radio's powerful media status.

LORD REITH
First director-general of the BBC was John Reith, who served until 1938. He set very high standards in all areas of radio broadcasting.

COMING OF COMMERCIALS

The US corporation AT&T established Radio WEAF in New York in 1922. It brought a new trend – commercials. The first was a ten-minute speech on behalf of real estate agents Queensborough Corporation, and it cost $50. In 1923, WEAF made an incredible profit of $150,000, and the radio business went into a big-time boom.

NETWORK BOSS
William Paley, seen here at the BBC, developed US radio network CBS into a multi-million-dollar business. He was chairman until 1946.

STILL AT WORK
Original inventor of practical radio, Guglielmo Marconi, set up successful radio businesses. His American Marconi company was bought by RCA in 1919.

DIFFERENT APPROACH

British radio developed in a different direction. The BBC (British Broadcasting Corporation) began as a private concern in 1922, with a news bulletin from Marconi House in The Strand, London on 14 November. In 1927, the BBC received a charter from the British government, allowing it to become totally independent. It was 'to educate, to entertain and to inform.' It was also to remain unaffected by pressure from politicians, governments and businesses, and receive no money from commercials.

NETWORK RIVALS

RCA (Radio Corporation of America), set up as a radio technology company, began its broadcasting network NBC (National Broadcasting Company) in 1926, under control of David Sarnoff. The rival CBS (Columbia Broadcasting System) was founded in 1927 and grew rapidly under William Paley (above).

Reading the NBC news, in 1935.

HOW RADIO WORKS

Radio waves are made of both electrical and magnetic energy. They are invisible and are broadcast (sent out) by a transmitter, from a wire called an aerial. The waves are picked up by a receiver – the 'radio set'.

MAKING WAVES

Radio uses a basic carrier wave that is altered, or modulated, to convey information in the form of a pattern or code. The first broadcasts used AM, where the height (amplitude) of the waves was altered. By 1933, US radio engineer Edwin Armstrong had invented FM, where the number of waves per second (frequency) was modulated. This produced clearer sounds and was less affected by weather.

Transmitter

Radio waves

AM/FM

Continuous carrier wave

AM, amplitude modulated wave

FM, frequency modulated wave

FAST AS LIGHT

Radio waves are similar in nature to light waves, and travel as quickly. Also they are largely unaffected by day or night, rain or clouds. So they are ideal for carrying information almost instantly. During the 1920s, scientists developed more powerful transmitters, to send or broadcast the waves over greater distances, from long aerial wires on tall poles. Smaller aerial poles began to appear on houses, to pick up the radio waves and feed them to the receiver or 'wireless equipment'.

RELAY STATIONS
Radio relay stations picked up broadcasts from far away, boosted their strength, and sent them onwards.

'SIMPLE RADIO MUSIC BOX'

In 1916, David Sarnoff, who became president of RCA (see page 9), suggested that radio would become a major medium for news and entertainment. He foresaw speech and music brought into every home through 'a simple music radio box'. Only ten years later, sales of these boxes, or radio sets, were rocketing. There were two main kinds. The crystal set needed little or no electricity supply, but it only had enough volume for a set of headphones. The valve set had electronic triode valves which increased the strength of the signals enough to drive a loudspeaker, but it needed a powerful electricity supply.

MORE VOLUME
The RadiAir receiver of 1925–26 had five valves for extra volume and a horn-shaped speaker.

'PORTABLE' RADIO?
In 1922, the BTH receiver was one of the world's smallest! Also it did not need a long aerial wire.

FIGHT NIGHT LIVE!
In 1920, most sports fans had to read about events next day in the paper. Radio brought news and commentary as they happened. One of the first big sports events heard live on the radio was the world heavyweight boxing championship between Jack Dempsey and George Carpenter, on 2 July 1921. It was also the first million-dollar boxing event.

'Dempsey has a knockout in the fourth round!'

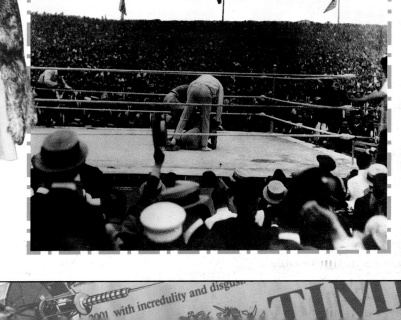

FEEDING THE AIRWAVES

From the 1920s, radio enjoyed its 'Golden Age'. This lasted until the 1950s and the growth of another new medium, television. The range of radio programmes widened from news and music to include current affairs, dramas, sports, comedy and light entertainment.

NON-STOP NEWS

One of radio's early great events was the first solo trans-Atlantic flight by US aviator Charles Lindbergh, in 1927. Such international news would usually be sent 'on the wires' (by telegraph) for reporting in newspapers. But this time the world waited by their radios for news of sightings of the lone flier – who, oddly, did not have a radio in his plane. After a 33-hour trip, listeners heard of Lindbergh's landing in Paris 'live'. The USA celebrated a new national hero before the newspapers could print the story.

TOP OF THE RATINGS

In commercial radio, adverts were priced according to the popularity of a programme. The first ratings to give official estimated numbers of listeners were produced in the USA by Crossley Inc. in 1930. The most popular show was NBC's *Amos 'n' Andy*.

WALTER WINCHELL (1897–1952) *Winchell's fast-talking, breathless, deadpan style influenced many announcers. His radio audience reached 20 million.*

AMOS 'N' ANDY *Freeman Gosden and Charles Correll were a popular comedy duo in theatres, and from 1929 on radio. They had 40 million listeners.*

12

WAR OF THE WORLDS

On 30 October 1938, Orson Welles broadcast a spoof Halloween version of the H. G. Wells story. A million Americans believed Martians had invaded, and panicked in the streets.

FAMILIAR VOICES

The first radio stars soon became known by their catch-phrases. US journalist Walter Winchell wrote 'gossip columns' for newspapers. In 1932, he adapted the idea for radio and began his networked Sunday night show with the phrase: 'Good evening, Mr and Mrs America, and all the ships at sea.' Early radio comedy stars included Jack Benny, George Burns and Gracie Allen.

LOSS OF THE HINDENBERG

In May 1937, the giant passenger airship Hindenberg *exploded in New Jersey, USA. Radio announcers were overwhelmed and reduced to tears.*

THE FIRST 'SOAPS'

The long-running drama serials known as 'soap operas' had their origins on radio in the late 1920s. During the daytime, many people listened to the radio at home, while doing housework. Makers of soaps, polishes, cleaners and similar domestic products recognized this, and began to advertise. Soon they were sponsoring whole shows.

A newspaper version of a soap advert.

IVORY SOAP

TV'S FALSE START

By the early 1920s, 'wireless' radio was sending speech, music and other sounds instantly over great distances. It was the new, exciting and fast-expanding medium. But inventors were already wondering: if radio waves could carry sounds, could they carry moving pictures as well?

BAIRD
John Logie Baird looks down the picture tube at the scanning Nipkow disc, on one of his early pieces of equipment.

A TESTING TIME

In 1924, still photographs were first sent from New York to London, as coded patterns of radio waves. This was a fast way of sending pictures for newspapers. But radio could broadcast sounds 'live' and continuously, as they happened. The aim was to do the same with the pictures as well as sounds.

GHOSTLY FACE
Baird's 1926 test transmissions sent pictures just a metre or two by radio waves. Each picture had 30 scanned lines and 10 pictures were shown each second. The pictures merged to give the impression of movement.

START OF A BUSINESS

By 1927, Baird was sending pictures between cities, with the scanning disc as the 'camera'. He also worked on colour and big-screen television. He even recorded TV programmes on discs similar to those used for sound recording. Although his system faded out, Baird helped to establish that television had a huge future as 'the next big medium'.

City-to-city television, 1927.

SPINNING DISC

Scottish electrical engineer John Logie Baird (1888–1946) was already working on this. From 1922, he improved a system first devised by Paul Nipkow in the 1880s. It used a fast-rotating 'scanning' disc with slots or holes (see opposite). In 1926, Baird sent his first test moving images by 'wireless vision' (television), a short distance between attic rooms in Soho, London. The face on the dim, fuzzy screen was that of a boy who just happened to be passing.

BAIRD AT THE BBC
By 1936, the BBC was broadcasting pictures using a Baird system with 240 lines. This gave the images higher definition – that is, made them sharper and clearer.

TUNING IN
John Logie Baird tunes an early 'wireless vision receiver' or TV set. However, by 1936 the BBC was deciding to switch to the rival all-electronic version (see page 16).

IMPROVEMENTS

In 1927 Baird transmitted his televisual pictures by phone line from London to Glasgow, and the next year, from London to New York. In 1929, he began test broadcasts for the BBC in London – half an hour each day of sound and vision, both carried by radio waves. Baird's success continued for another few years. But it was a false start. By 1936, all-electronic systems took over.

EARLY TELEVISION CAMERA

Spinning Nipkow disc
Light through hole
Focusing lens
Spot of light reflects off object
Bright light source
Gate
To transmitter
Photo cells detect light spots

In Baird's system, a disc with a spiral of holes rotated to allow tiny spots of light to shine through in fast succession. The spots were aimed to move up, down and across the object, to 'scan' it. Each spot's brightness was changed into a corresponding electrical pulse by photocells. The receiver worked in reverse, projecting moving spots of light of varying brightness on to a screen. But the process was limited by wear and tear on its moving parts, and the need to adjust both sending and receiving discs with extreme precision.

Image as seen on screen.

FLICKERING SCREEN

Today's major medium is television. Life without it may be difficult to imagine. Its story began in the 1920s, as an experimental curiosity. By the 1930s, it was found in a few homes, mainly of the rich and famous. But its progress was delayed partly by World War Two (1939–45). Television started to become common in ordinary homes in the 1950s.

TV CAMERA
The BBC began all-electronic broadcasts in 1936. In 1938, it set up television studios at Alexandra Palace (shown in the background) in North London.

INVISIBLE BEAM

As John Logie Baird worked on his part-mechanical television system (see previous page), a Russian-born American was developing a version with no moving parts. Vladimir Zworykin used an invisible beam of tiny particles called electrons, which are parts of atoms. This was produced inside a device called a cathode ray tube, invented in 1897.

A view future TV from 19

TV HQ

At the BBC's Alexandra Palace, programmes were sent out using an electronic system similar to Zworykin's, devised by Marconi-EMI. The screen had 405 horizontal lines. Tests on practical colour television began in 1940.

VISION FOR VISION

David Sarnoff, head of RCA (see page 9), saw that TV could be an important medium – and a profitable one. He invested $50 million in Zworykin's work.

ZWORYKIN (1889–1982)

Vladimir Zworykin developed his first electronic television system while working at Westinghouse in 1923. He called the tube an iconoscope.

17

OLD TUBE, NEW USE

Zworykin made the tube's front into a screen. Electrons from a 'gun' inside the back of the tube hit the inside of the screen, which was coated in dots of a substance called phosphor. This glowed when hit by electrons. The beam moved or scanned down the screen, line by line, and the glowing dots built up pictures that changed so fast, movement seemed continuous. This process is still the basis of today's standard TV set.

BIG MONEY

In Britain, Marconi-EMI were developing similar equipment. Test systems were demonstrated in 1932, and the BBC began regular broadcasts in 1936. But general progress continued to be slow. In 1939, RCA showed Franklin D. Roosevelt speaking at the World Fair in New York – the first US presidential broadcast.

WHAT FUTURE FOR TV?

In the late 1920s, as television programmes began in patchy areas, news spread of this strange new medium. Would it be a success? The screens of early TV receivers were small, dim and blurred, and hardly seemed worth the bother of viewing. Radio sets were much easier to use, and there were far more programmes.

AT THE MOVIES

By 1920, cinema was established as a major medium for entertainment. There was no television, and radio was in its infancy. Going to the movies became a way of escaping from daily routine and life's problems.

'TINSEL TOWN' – HOLLYWOOD

In 1911, the first movie studios had been established in Hollywood, a district of the US city of Los Angeles. By 1920, Hollywood ruled the American movie business. It was also coming to dominate other regions where films were popular, especially Europe. Ordinary people had enough money to go to the movies, and cinema as a medium grew in influence. What the major stars wore, said and did, and even their hairstyles and mannerisms, were copied by people in everyday life.

SILENT FUN

Comedy stars of the era included Buster Keaton and here, Harold Lloyd in Safety Last (1923). Lloyd climbs a skyscraper for his girlfriend. His movies were filled with ever more amazing stunts.

INHUMAN FUTURE

Metropolis (1926), *by German director Fritz Lang, told a story of robot-like workers in a future factory. Its weird scenes were influenced by artistic trends in painting, sculpture, poetry and even furniture design.*

FACT AND FICTION

At first, there were worries that movie-goers might confuse screen events with daily reality. But fears were unfounded, and cinema flourished. Comedy was king, led by Charlie Chaplin in *The Kid* (1921) and *The Gold Rush* (1925). Different kinds or genres of films emerged. There were American adventures in the 'Wild West' with *The Covered Wagon* (1923), religious epics such as *The Ten Commandments* (1923) and war stories like *The Big Parade* (1925).

AT THE FOREFRONT

European cinema was less concerned with realistic stories, and more with art and impressions. In the vast newly-formed nation of the USSR, Sergei Eisenstein's *Battleship Potemkin* (1925) showed many innocent people dying during the Russian revolution.

19

FILMING REAL LIFE
Documentaries record real life as it happens, without interference from movie-makers. The idea began in 1921 with a 57-minute film by Robert Flaherty about the life of an Inuit (then called Eskimo) family, *Nanook of the North*. Documentaries soon became a popular form of cinema. Today most are shown on television.

Tragically, Nanook died on the ice, soon after the film was made.

THE BIG STUDIOS
Huge film companies, called studios, built vast movie-making centres around Los Angeles, California. Each studio signed a group of stars and there was cut-throat competition to produce more successful releases.

YOU AIN'T HEARD NOTHING

At first, movies were silent. Some had music in the background, usually from a pianist or other live musicians, or from a recording on disc. But there were no sounds directly from the action happening on the screen. Then, in 1927…

ALL TALK

The first film with a full-length soundtrack was Lights of New York (1928) starring Helene Costello and Cullen Landis. It was an early example of the gangster movie, when a dancer becomes mixed up with big-time criminals.

MUSICALS

The arrival of 'talking pictures' led to a 1930s boom in musicals. The Wizard of Oz (1939) won an Oscar award for the song 'Over the Rainbow' and was also one of the first Technicolor movies.

OVERNIGHT SENSATION

Warner Brothers' *The Jazz Singer* created an instant sensation. At one point the star, singer-actor Al Jolson, said 'You ain't heard nothin'!' The words seemed to come directly from his lips. Audiences were astonished. The name 'talkies' was given to films with sound locked into, or synchronized with, screen action.

The Jazz Singer was partly silent. But it had four musical sequences and some spoken lines. The sounds came from a disc recording which was precisely linked to the film projector, known as the Vitaphone system (see page 22).

NO SQUEAKIES

Cinema critic Welford Beaton wrote in *The Film Spectator*: 'If I were an actor with a squeaky voice, I would worry.' He was right. Within a year of *The Jazz Singer*'s release, silent movies were almost dead. Stars had to have attractive voices as well as acting skills. However, technical difficulties of recording soundtracks took the attention of film-makers away from the visual side. Audiences complained that 'motion pictures' seemed to contain few interesting pictures and little motion.

FILMING THE NEWS

Before television became widespread, people could see the news in moving pictures at the cinema. Important events were filmed and then shown on newsreels, often as a short feature before the main movie. Film cameras joined the rows of stills photographers from newspapers, to record the latest events. Newsreels often became 'raw material' for film-makers, as famous events were made into motion pictures.

Large movie cameras among the newspaper photographers.

DANCERS AND GANGSTERS

In the 1930s, Hollywood's list of world-famous stars seemed endless: Greta Garbo, Marlene Dietrich, Mae West, Bette Davis, Cary Grant, Gary Cooper and Clark Gable. Fred Astaire and Ginger Rogers 'danced on air' in *Top Hat* (1935). James Cagney was *The Public Enemy* (1931) in a new style of film, the gangster movie, inspired by the era of prohibition and liquor bootlegging in the USA.

RISKY SCENE
There were few special effects in the 1930s. Even the roaring lion, symbol of MGM Studios, was filmed 'live'.

SOUNDS OF MUSIC

The medium of recorded sound had risen in popularity since the invention of mass-produced flat discs in 1901, by Emile Berliner. Sales of discs rose steadily as more people bought the machines to play them on, called gramophones.

A 1933 radio factory.

DISC CHECK
In the gramophone disc, sounds were coded as a wavy groove which spiralled into the centre. Most recordings lasted just five minutes.

SOUNDTRACK
For the first few years of talking pictures, the soundtrack was on a gramophone-type disc. This one is being checked under the microscope for flaws and other problems.

LIGHT SOUND
This 1935 cinema projector could play soundtracks recorded on disc or as patterns of light alongside the movie images. The second system gradually took over.

NOT JUST MUSIC

By the 1920s sound recordings included, not only songs and music, but also famous speeches, poetry, plays and dramas. But in the 1930s, disc sales fell rapidly. The main reason for this was that radio provided all of the above types of sounds. And after buying the radio receiver, it was 'free'.

TUMBLING PRICES

In the 1920s, the prices of gramophones, radios and similar equipment began to fall. It was partly a result of mass production on assembly lines. This method had been invented in 1913 by the Ford Motor Company, to make cars. Also radio broadcasting companies encouraged sales, so that more people would fall under the influence of their medium.

SOUNDTRACKS

By 1930 all movies had soundtracks. Why pay for a disc of songs, when you could hear them and also see them performed, at the cinema? The recorded music industry shifted to working on musical films, using singing stars of the silver screen. However records of orchestras, classical music and operas continued to sell well. Such works featured less in movies or on radio.

GOING ELECTRIC

Advances in recorded sound technology were also linked to radio and cinema. At first, movie audiences had to sit near gramophone-type sound horns while watching the screen. Engineers began to use electricity to increase, or amplify, the volume. The electro-magnetic loudspeaker still used today was developed by General Electric in the late 1920s. The first practical high-volume speakers were in cinemas by about 1935.

TAPE RECORDERS

The first 'tape' recorders actually used wires to store sound patterns as magnetic patches. Flexible tape with a thin iron coating was developed by BASF in 1936.

THE MICROPHONE

The first microphones date from about 1925. Sound waves hitting a diaphragm (flexible sheet) make a wire coil vibrate near a magnet, which produces varying electrical signals. Before this, performers had to cluster around a funnel-shaped horn, and quiet sounds were usually lost.

Sound waves

Diaphragm

Wire coil

Magnet

Electrical signals

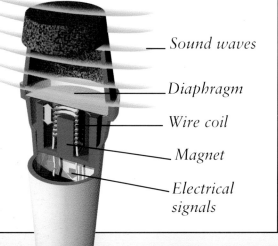

STEREO

Bell Laboratories' 'Oscar' tested stereo from 1931. Each ear receives slightly different sounds, for greater all-round realism.

PRINT WARS

The word 'tabloid' was invented in 1884, for a small package containing medicine – a tablet. But by 1920 it had become the name for another small 'package' which contained the day's news. This was the tabloid newspaper.

EASIER TO READ

One of the first major tabloid newspapers was the *London Daily Mirror*. It was started in 1903 by Alfred Harmsworth, who became Lord Northcliffe. When he died in 1922, the paper was selling well over one million copies daily. The tabloid was smaller than most other papers, which were known as broadsheets. It had big headlines, large pictures and easy-to-read text focusing on sensational and human-interest stories.

24

PRESS BARONS
Daily Mirror founder Lord Northcliffe (left), his brother and successor Lord Rothermere (right), and a third brother.

ON THE STREET
Telephones, radio and faster printing presses meant that papers could be reporting an event such as a sports match, within an hour of its finish. These vendors are from 1934.

GROWING TREND

Lord Northcliffe was succeeded by his brother Harold, who became Lord Rothermere. Their Amalgamated Press company was the biggest print media group of the time. The idea of the inexpensive tabloid newspaper spread rapidly to Europe and the USA. Joseph Patterson founded the *New York Daily News* in 1919. This was followed by the *Evening Graphic* and the US *Daily Mirror*, which were both started in 1924.

INSTANT REPORT
Reporters phoned in their stories in sections, such as at half-time in a sports event. This saved precious minutes to beat rival papers.

TOWER OF POWER

Newspapers were read by millions of people daily, so they had tremendous influence in the stories they covered and the opinions they expressed. They could not compete with the new medium of radio for speed when first announcing or 'breaking' a story. So many papers turned to more in-depth, detailed analysis of events – 'looking behind the news'. Their editorial columns, letters and feature articles allowed various people to express differing viewpoints. The *New York Times*, founded in 1851, rose to be the most respected daily newspaper in the USA.

The prestigious offices of the New York Times, *1924.*

JAZZ JOURNALISM

One simple benefit of the tabloid was its small size. People could open it and read it more easily on crowded buses and trains. The short, snappy, drama-packed reporting style with numerous pictures became known as 'jazz journalism'. The larger-format broadsheets, with their longer, in-depth reports, complained that tabloids did not take world events seriously. But tabloids helped to maintain the popularity of newspapers as a medium in the face of the radio boom.

SMILE, PLEASE
Many reporters and photographers were from press agencies. They gathered the news, took the pictures, and sold them to the newspapers.

LIFE AND TIME

During the 1920s, several new types of magazines began to change the style of publishing. Most originated in the USA and spread across to Europe. These publications included *Time*, *Life* and the 'pocket periodical' *Reader's Digest*.

BURSTING WITH MAGAZINES
During the 1930s, city news-stands were swamped by new magazines and journals. Many were aimed at people travelling to and from work.

TIME MARCHES ON
Henry Luce (1898–1967) adapted the format of Time *as a radio programme and then a film series,* The March of Time.

26

HISTORIC COVER
This edition of Life *was the first after its re-launch. The above edition of* Fortune *deals with photography.*

FOR BUSY READERS

The leading publisher behind this new style of magazine was Henry Luce. With his colleague Briton Hadden, he began *Time* in 1923. It was a weekly news summary, written for the more educated public, with many high-quality pictures. Its contents were organized into easy-to-follow sections to help the busy reader. The USA was entering the Depression but *Time* was a huge success and in 1930 Luce launched a second magazine, *Fortune*. *Life* followed in 1935–36. It became the biggest seller of all weekly picture magazines.

PHOTO-JOURNALISM

Life had been a satire-based periodical since 1883. Luce bought it in 1935 and re-launched it as the magazine for readers who wanted 'to see life; to see the world; to eyewitness great events.' The news was told largely in photographs with explanatory captions, a medium known as photo-journalism. Luce's political views were very conservative and very anti-communist. He used his editor-in-chief position, his money and his publications to influence public mood, and to affect the US government's views on various communist nations.

PAPERBACKS
Penguin Books changed people's view of the book with their paperbacks. (Nine of the first ten are shown here.) Books suddenly became cheap enough for anyone to buy.

A NOVEL IDEA

Penguin began a new trend in books in 1936, when they launched paperbacks. Most books at the time were hardbacks, expensive to buy and often valued more for their leather covers and quality binding than for their contents. Paperbacks were inexpensive, read-anywhere, throw-away novels – and an instant success.

PICTURES RULE
The 1930s trend for illustrated magazines spread to many countries. This is a 1932 edition of the French L'Illustré.

HOW SMALL BECAME HUGE
Reader's Digest was founded in the USA in 1920–22 by former book salesman DeWitt Wallace and his wife Lila Acheson. Its approach was to take news, features and articles that were printed elsewhere, and make them into shorter, condensed summaries or 'digests'. *Reader's Digest* was aimed at people who wanted to read a variety of topics quickly, yet still find the important information. In size, it was small enough to slip into a coat pocket. It grew into one of the world's most successful publications.

DeWitt (1889–1981) and Lila (1889–1984).

THE READER'S DIGEST

31 ARTICLES EACH MONTH FROM LEADING MAGAZINES, EACH ARTICLE OF ENDURING VALUE AND INTEREST, IN CONDENSED AND PERMANENT FORM.

January, 1920

WORLD AT WAR

As the 1930s progressed, the newspapers, radio and other media had no shortage of events to report. Wars and conflicts broke out in many parts of the world. In 1939 came the news that many dreaded. Another World War had begun.

GROWING UNEASE

Adolf Hitler had become leader of Germany in 1933. He built up the country's military forces as his Nazi movement gained strength (see page 6). Nations such as France, Britain and the USA remained neutral, trying to avoid all-out war. However, in 1938, German forces invaded Austria. The American radio reporter Edward Murrow gave a sombre account of Hitler's arrival in the Austrian capital, Vienna. Millions of listeners began to realize for the first time that the Nazi campaign was an urgent threat to world peace.

KEEPING IN TOUCH
Many children were sent away from unsafe areas. They kept in touch with home through newspapers.

In this momentous photograph, British prime minister Neville Chamberlain waves an agreement from Hitler to cease military activity in Europe. Within a year, World War Two had begun.

WAR REPORTERS
Edward Murrow (on the right), here with colleague William Shirer, was the leading war correspondent of his time. His reports were concise and accurate, and managed to convey the horror of battle.

THE PROPAGANDA WAR

Compared to World War One, media reporting of World War Two was generally more open, accurate and faster. Radio links could flash news in both words and pictures across continents in seconds. Nations listened to each other's programmes. Some even broadcast direct to the enemy. Listeners were told that their country was not fighting a just cause and it could never win the war, so the best choice was to surrender at once. This type of selective, biased information, produced specially to push forward or propagate a cause, is known as propaganda. It flourishes during wartime.

EMOTIONAL SCENES
This poster by Pierre Mail portrays suffering of left-wing activists under the right-wing Fascists during the Spanish Civil War (1936–39).

Chinese posters honour their glorious army.

CONFLICT IN THE EAST
World War Two quickly spread to East Asia. From the late 1920s in Japan, military officers had been seizing senior government positions. They used newspapers, radio, movies and other media to celebrate Japan's great military history. People were told that their nation would soon rise again as a major world power. As a result, public support for conflict grew. In 1937, Japan attacked China. In 1940, it signed military agreements with Germany and Italy, and the war raged.

GLOSSARY

BROADCAST MEDIA News and information sent out to many people – that is, broadcast – usually in the form of radio (electromagnetic) waves, as radio and TV programmes.

DIAPHRAGM A thin, flexible sheet or plate that can vibrate easily, used in microphones.

PHOTO-JOURNALISM Conveying information such as a news story or report using primarily photographs with captions, rather than mainly written text with accompanying pictures.

PRESS A machine (printing press) that prints newspapers, books and similar items. Also a general term for reporters, journalists, interviewers and other people gathering information for the media.

PRINT MEDIA News and information printed or otherwise put on to paper, as in books, magazines, journals, newspapers and posters.

RADIO The general name for the sound-only medium which uses invisible electromagnetic waves sent out, or broadcast, from transmitter to receiver. 'A radio' is also the everyday name for a radio receiver or radio set.

TABLOID A newspaper with a small format (page size), smaller than a broadsheet but larger than a typical magazine. The term also refers to the style of journalism using large headlines, lots of pictures, and easy-to-read text written in a vivid or sensational style.

TELEGRAPHY 'Writing at a distance', a system of changing written words or other marks on paper into codes of electrical signals and sending them along wires or cables.

TELEPHONE 'Speaking at a distance', a system of changing spoken words or other sounds into codes of electrical signals and sending them along wires or cables.

VALVE An electronic device which looks like a small glass tube with metal parts (electrodes) inside. Valves have various jobs, such as using a very small, varying electric current to control a much larger current.

WIRELESS An early nickname for radio. Unlike the telegraph or telephone, the sender and receiver were not linked by wires, and so the system was said to be 'wire-less'. Also the name for an early radio set.

WORLD EVENTS

- Women over 21 get the vote in USA — 1
- Communist Party founded in China — 1
- Russia and others found USSR — 1
- Mussolini seizes power in Italy — 1
- First Labour government for Britain — 1
- Albania gains independence — 1
- Military takeover in Poland — 1
- Russia: power struggle with Stalin and Trotsky — 1
- Hoover becomes US President — 1
- 'Apartheid' begins in South Africa — 1
- Japan's prime minister Hamaguchi assassinated — 1
- Revolution as Spain becomes a republic — 1
- French President Doumer assassinated — 1
- Hitler takes control in Germany — 1
- Dust Bowl destroys US farmlands — 1
- Italy invades Abyssinia (now Ethiopia) — 1
- Spanish Civil War begins — 1
- Japan attacks China — 1
- Germany invades Austria — 1
- World War Two begins — 1

TIMELINE

	HEADLINES	MEDIA EVENTS	MEDIA TECH	PERFORMANCE & ART
0	•Joan of Arc becomes a saint	•Reader's Digest small-format magazine begins	•First radio station licences in USA	•Stravinsky's Pulcinella ballet with voices
1	•The Sheik makes Rudolf Valentino a world star	•First big sports events heard live on radio	•Baird begins early tests on scan-disc TV system	•Charlie Chaplin: The Kid •Documentary: Nanook
2	•Press baron Lord Northcliffe dies	•New York's Radio WEAF begins commercials	•BBC's first broadcasts from Marconi House	•Murnau's Nosferatu, an early horror film
3	•First soccer FA Cup Final at Wembley	•Time magazine founded by Luce and Hadden	•Zworykin works on all-electronic TV system	•Huge-budget The Ten Commandments (de Mille)
4	•USSR: Lenin dies, mourning / celebration	•USA: Evening Graphic and Daily Mirror papers	•Photos sent trans-Atlantic as coded radio signals	•Surrealist style of painting gains prominence
5	•Charleston dance craze	•The Times: Saturday front page on Monday too	•Early microphones appear	•Eisenstein: Battleship Potemkin (Russian film)
6	•General Strike in Britain	•USA: NBC network is founded	•Baird transmits first TV images by radio	•Fritz Lang: Metropolis
7	•Lindbergh flies solo non-stop across Atlantic	•USA: CBS network is founded	•BBC is given charter of independence	•Jolson speaks from the screen in The Jazz Singer
8	•Amelia Earhart, first woman to fly Atlantic	•Mickey Mouse hits the big screen	•First all-soundtrack movies	•Surrealism in film with Un Chien Andalou (Dali)
9	•USA: Wall Street Crash and Depression begins	•USA: Amos 'n' Andy begin radio shows	•Baird begins test TV programmes, London	•New York: Museum of Modern Art founded
0	•Ghandi leads protest marches in India	•Fortune magazine begins	•Radio ratings system to estimate listener numbers	•Noel Coward: Private Lives
1	•New York: Empire State Building finished	•TV outside broadcast of the Derby horse race, UK	•The Times Weekly Edition goes full colour	•Bela Lugosi stars in Dracula
2	•Roosevelt becomes US President	•Walter Winchell begins his radio show	•BBC moves to London's Broadcasting House	•First of the Tarzan feature films
3	•USA: Prohibition ends	•King Kong begins new era of special effects	•Armstrong develops FM radio	•Queen Christina stars 'ice beauty' Garbo
4	•China: Mao and Long March		•Cinemas begin to use large loudspeakers	•Shirley Temple, aged 6, wins film Oscar
5	•M. Campbell's land speed record, 484 km/h	•Life magazine begins limited test publications	•Technicolor developed for movies	•Rogers and Astaire dance in Top Hat
6	•Berlin Olympics •Edward VIII abdicates	•BBC begins regular TV broadcasts, England	•Flexible magnetic tape for sound recordings (BASF)	•Penguin launches paperback novels
7	•Hindenberg airship explodes near New York	•Radio pioneer Marconi dies	•Reporters benefit from new pen: the biro	•Disney's first feature animation Snow White
8	•War of the Worlds on radio causes mass panic	•Reith retires as director-general of the BBC	•BBC sets up TV studios at Alexandra Palace	•Recumbent Figure, sculpture by Henry Moore
9	•World Fair, New York •Spanish Civil War ends	•Roosevelt is first US President to appear on TV	•Colour TV tests show it will be practical	•The Wizard of Oz in Technicolor

INDEX